There's a Hum

poems by

Jeanne-Marie Osterman

Finishing Line Press
Georgetown, Kentucky

There's a Hum

Copyright © 2018 by Jeanne-Marie Osterman
ISBN 978-1-63534-389-2 First Edition
All rights reserved under International and Pan-American Copyright Conventions. No part of this book may be reproduced in any manner whatsoever without written permission from the publisher, except in the case of brief quotations embodied in critical articles and reviews.

ACKNOWLEDGMENTS

I am grateful to the editors of the publications in which the following poems have appeared, sometimes in slightly different forms:

Bluestem: "Boxwoods"
California Quarterly: "Hospital Gardens"
The Madison Review: "Horny Goat Weed"
The RavensPerch: "Having What You Don't Remember," "Reports from Sierra Leone," "Cracked," "Assisted Living"
Third Wednesday: "Malika"

Thanks to the friends and teachers who encouraged me.

Thanks to The Writers Room, New York City, for providing me with the time and space.

Above all, love and thanks to you, Harold.

Publisher: Leah Maines

Editor: Christen Kincaid

Cover Art and Design: Maria Vargas DeStefano

Author Photo: Anonymous

Printed in the USA on acid-free paper.
Order online: www.finishinglinepress.com
also available on amazon.com

Author inquiries and mail orders:
Finishing Line Press
P. O. Box 1626
Georgetown, Kentucky 40324
U. S. A.

Table of Contents

Cracked 1
A History of Survival 2
Bob 3
Theater of War 4
A Thank You Note from My Father 5
Horny Goat Weed 6
Reports from Sierra Leone 7
Docked 8
Canyon Creek Logging, 1937 9
For I Will Sing of Telephone Wires 10
Candlesticks 11
What Goes On in the Town Hidden Behind
   the Trees of the Tree-Lined Interstate 12
Boxwoods 13
Having What You Don't Remember 14
The Guatemalan Bus 15
Malika 16
Disclaimers 17
How to Shrink Your Own Head 19
The Reading 20
On the Number 6 21
Snowfall 22
Things You Can Do with a Heart 23
Hospital Gardens 24
Assisted Living 25
Natural Aging Process 26
Elegy 27
Every Year 'Bout This Time 28

CRACKED

I can take you Tuesday,
the doctor said over the heads
of three interns he'd brought in
to see my film. They were gaping
at an x-ray of my pelvis, their mouths
open wide as the butterfly wings of my torn ilium—
a Rorschach betraying central instability.
If the breach grows any wider, they say,
I'll fall apart completely—
collapse like a limp doll.
The plan is to graft a cadaver's bone
onto mine, the arranged marriage
to be performed under a canopy
of blue surgical plastic, the union
secured with tiny pins and glue
in hopes we two
will be compatible and bond
for life. Some easy walks
in the park at first,

then, maybe dancing.

A HISTORY OF SURVIVAL

When I saw you hunkered
in the weeds at the Darwin Center
craning your neck from your hard carapace
I thought of the ancient fable where you
raced the hare and how your history has been
one long contest against pirates and conquistadors
who, laughing like hares on race day, bagged you
by the thousands, ripped the shells off your backs
and hacked them into guitar picks and trinkets
for their ladies' hair. Here at the Darwin Center
tourists snap you with their digi-cams
laughing at the way you copulate—
a long slow process of grunts
and mournful thrusts.

BOB

Bob sits on the porch swing
drawing on an unfiltered Camel.
Bob blows a stream of smoke rings
into the warm Tennessee night air.

The rings bring a kind of peace—
a peace good enough for him.

Bob is thinking about that night in Nam.
It was quiet just like this. Humid
just like this. Trees rustled just like this.

Bob's lungs rumble with the next pull.
His Purple Heart rests in a drawer upstairs.
Next to it, the night school certificate
that got him on at Three Mile Island.

When Unit Two blew, Bob
went to war again. Climbing the reactor
in a foil suit. Carrying torch and wrench.

More rings drift from the porch.
They glide through the air like ghosts.

THEATER OF WAR

"Here's how it looked after the kamikaze hit,"
my father says, holding the cruise book in his lap.

The Japanese plane looks like a ball
of crumpled paper on the ship's massive deck.

Next to the wreckage, eleven mummies
wrapped in white canvas and the American flag.

KEEP OFF is written in white chalk along their feet.
"One at a time we put them on a table. We used

a mess hall table. We weighted each one
with a canon ball and tipped it into the sea."

A THANK YOU NOTE FROM MY FATHER

Dear Jeannie,

I received the book, *Ardennes 1944*, in the mail yesterday.
I know I will enjoy it very much.

I remember when this was going on. It was Christmas day.
I was stationed at Camp Elliott. I was standing in the chow
line. I was reading the newspaper about what was going
on in Ardennes.

I was waiting for my dinner— turkey and all that good stuff.

A week later I was headed for Okinawa. I had an interesting job—
going through the stuff of the guys who got killed, throwing out
items like letters or pictures that might be offensive to wives or
parents and shipping what was left back home.

Thank you for this wonderful book.

Love,
JDO

HORNY GOAT WEED

I'm cleaning the kitchenette of my dad's studio
at the retirement villa where he's agreed to live out his days.

I'm dusting the pharmacopeia that keeps him alive
when I see the bottle of Horny Goat Weed.

I'm in Dad's bathroom typing the name into my phone.
I'm reading it's a remedy for erectile dysfunction—

Take two prior to activity; if desired, take up to three.
My dad's ninety-six. My mom's been dead for years.

When I come out of the bathroom, I see Dad's put
the Horny Goat Weed in the trash. Of course, I pretend

not to notice. When I get home, I take out all the self-help
books I have hidden under my bed. *Conquering Guilt,*

Hiding Shame, Looking for Love. I stack them
in the refrigerator for the next person needing milk to read.

REPORTS FROM SIERRA LEONE
after Afaa Michael Weaver

It's like a game of whack-a-mole,
the newspaper says. Public health
workers are pictured on page one.
In cloaks of blue plastic, moon
boots and monster goggles,
they look like ghosts.

Over twelve hundred dead in Sierra Leone

They go from village to village
and house to house hunting down
the afflicted. They take them to
treatment centers where there is
no cure. No one will bury the bodies,
the newspaper says. The virus still
dances on top of the corpse, turning
grave diggers into new partners.

Over three thousand dead in Sierra Leone

A Mr. Mohammed Kamara comes forward.
Someone has to do it, he says. He buries
over a thousand bodies. Ebola outbreak
officially over, the newspaper says today.
The orange plastic fencing that once cordoned
off a village loosens and waves in the breeze.

Over four thousand dead in Sierra Leone

DOCKED

The knife must have slipped when
they hacked off Buster's tail.
What's left doesn't cover much
back there. Nothing thumps
on the floor when we walk
in the door. The stub
flutters like a bug's wing.
Once I heard it buzz.
Buster, rudderless.
The phantom
limb stirs
the air.

CANYON CREEK LOGGING, 1937

In a hand-written letter, he tells me how it was
reeling in the moss-covered giants.
We didn't have roads or trucks out there.
We pulled the big cedars in by hand.

With a two-man handsaw the fallers fell the tree.
Choker-man sets hooks deep into the bark
then nods to the whistle punk
to yank the wire
that signals the yarder man
to fire up the steam donkey
that cranks the rig
that pulls the mainline
that hauls her in.

An 11 x 17 Xerox of one of the felled behemoths is attached.
The men perched on top look like ants.
My dad, third from the left, is only 18.
No lights, no phone, no hardhats, he's scrawled on the back.
The water was cold and piped from streams.

FOR I WILL SING OF TELEPHONE WIRES

For tethering me to nightstand, desk, and kitchen counter
For holding me in tight radius as horse to lunge line, dog to leash
For lengthy reminder of master at other end
For I wound you about my wrist in nervous twist
    waiting for a sign that I exist
For the marching orders, the answer, the verdict, the results
For word traveled fast through your snakelike coils
For you spilled like small talk over hardwood, linoleum
    and wall-to-wall
For this I shoved you under desk making nest for dust bunnies
    and mites who hunkered in your scattershot whorls
For you lay there like a lariat or a tumbleweed blown in from
    Arizona
For this I pinned you to the wall for fear I'd trip and fall
For this I hired a man with a gun
For this I paid by the hour
For you were stabbed with staples and coated with paint
For you were my private line and confidant
For we were so entwined. But it was not to last
For today you were ripped away
For you were bound, bagged, and driven to the town dump
For we have gone wireless now

CANDLESTICKS

I asked my new husband if we could have new candlesticks to replace the brass prickets his late wife had on the dining room table. Yes, he said, and he came shopping with me. We found three.

One stands on spindly legs like a spider. It holds a tiny candle where the spider's mouth would be. One is tall, matte black and curvy. It was designed by a woman who was accused of trying to assassinate Joseph Stalin. The third is very old. It holds the candle in a crude clip. There are holes where hot wax dripped down and wore through the metal.

We have our own collection now, my new husband and I. Three ways to hold the fire that lights our dinners each night. Looking into the flames snuffs out my curiosity of what may have burned here before.

WHAT GOES ON IN THE TOWN HIDDEN BEHIND THE TREES OF THE TREE-LINED INTERSTATE

Along Hwy 99 I see strip malls rising from wet pavement:
a tattoo parlor, a paint ball palace, the red neon of Chin's

Pavilion of the 10-Ingredient Lo Mein. Driver hunched
over fur-covered wheel, dirty dice dangling above

shaded eyes leers at me in my rental car. A patch of crab
grass bursts through the blacktop in search of sun—

weed I once plucked, sucked and cut a lip on, weed I
braided into a May crown to wear the day Jimmy Dawson

pumped his legs so hard he made the swing fly over the swing-
set— chains clanging as he hit the dirt, silence as they walked

him away like a criminal, arm hanging limp in plaid sleeve.
A horn blast brings me back to Hwy 99. Oxidized green

pick-up turns into a tavern. Debussy's *Sacred and Profane
Dances* plays on my radio. I am no longer young.

BOXWOODS

They're still there
lining the walk I
crawled fifty yrs
ago a girl in blue
overalls digging for

worms catching
beetles in mayo
jars salting the
occasional slug
watching it curl

to a slow death
learning how it
felt to be cruel.
They're still there
the gnarled brown

limbs twisting up
from the earth:
arthritic carnival
dancers in lush
green hats. The

peppery scent
taught me I had
senses, the con-
stant pruning
what life requires.

HAVING WHAT YOU DON'T REMEMBER

I hadn't seen my sister in years so when I got to town I took her to the mall where over cheese soup and a martini she tells me our grandpa murdered a man. It happened in South Dakota during the Great Depression.

Grandpa had a grocery store and there was an apple in the bin out front. An Indian off the reservation wandered by and when he thought no one was looking, put the apple in his pocket and walked away. Grandpa kept a loaded gun behind the counter and shot the Indian without warning— killed a man for taking an apple.

Not long after that, Grandpa moved the family out West where he thought they could have a better life. He was never charged with any crime.

He died before I was born but I'd always kept a picture of him on my mantle. After my sister told me this story, I put the picture in a drawer. I couldn't bring myself to look at it anymore. Nor could I bring myself to throw it away.

A poet I admire once said, "I have only what I remember." But I can't agree with him here. Because even though I never knew— and so could not possibly remember— my grandfather, I have him. He lives deep inside of me and he talks to me every day.

THE GUATEMALAN BUS

A man from Guatemala goes to Corpus Christi, Texas, to buy a used school bus at auction. The buses come from school districts all over the USA. They're still in good shape but, for reasons not entirely clear, the school districts feel they need to be replaced. The Guatemalan man buys one of the buses and drives it back to Antigua where it's retrofitted for the rugged Guatemalan highways. Then it's painted with flames, stars, tree branches, flowers, birds, butterflies, lizards, cartoon characters and stripes. The inside is decorated with holy pictures, medallions and prayer beads. So many beads are hung from the rear view mirror you wonder how the driver will see out. When the bus is finished, the local priest comes by with a silver baton full of holy water and shakes it on the bus, inside and out. The driver's family is there and the wife is crying because she knows her husband stands a good chance of being killed once he goes out on the road. What happens is, the *bandidos* get on and hold the driver at gunpoint. If he can't pay what they demand, usually several hundred dollars, they kill him. They leave the passengers on the road and take the bus to a garage where it's repainted and sold to another driver who repaints it again, has it decorated again, and blessed. Meanwhile, in the school district where the bus came from, the kids don't notice they're riding in a new bus.

MALIKA

It didn't feel
like anything
to be white
until I went
to Malika,
a sea village
in Senegal,
where a withered
old woman
in a black and yellow
boubou
came so close
I could smell her
chicken breath.
She laid her wash-
tub hand on my
sunburned arm,
fingered my
fine hair
and laughed.

DISCLAIMERS
anagrams

I.

the list is dismal
children get lice
the old go lame
life leaves scars
love gives AIDS
we're mired
in a sea
of litigious isms
that scare
us into reading mail
that raises
hopes then reads
you a lie

II.

first you hear the lies
then you read
what's real
a list of isms
to raise
a scare:
you may feel at sea
so dismal
you may maim
yourself or the dame
in the next aisle
skin crawls like lice
legs go lame
there could be scars
oh and die
they don't care
a cure is not their deal
their aim
is to sell the idea

III.

she aimed
to raid
my southern isle
drown me in a sea
of ideas
about maid-
enhood. I kept clam.
Dames
aren't my deal
I learned in my ism
it's a dismal
sin to get un clad
with any but a lad
I'll go mad
get lame
die
of AIDS
or a case
of lice
you're scared
my dear
she said

HOW TO SHRINK YOUR OWN HEAD

Make slit at back of neck.
        Pull flesh from
        cranium.
        Remove skull.

Hollow out what's left
        taking care
        to keep cartilage
        in place.

Sew eyelids shut.
        Fasten mouth with three
        sharp palm needles.
        (Big mouths may require more.)

Place wooden ball
        where brain was.
        Boil thirty minutes.
        Dry on hot rocks.

Rub exterior with ash
        to keep soul
        from seeping
        out.

You're going to need it
        now that you
        don't have
        a brain.

THE READING

Sharing a cab home
from poetry workshop,
somewhere near
the corner of Sixth
and Manhole Cover,
you pull a Mary Oliver
poem from your purse.
"This is beautiful," you say.
You want to read it to me
but it's late and dark
so you can only read
when the taxi stops
under a street lamp.
Lifting the page up
into the light
you read as much
as you can
until the taxi rolls
into darkness again.
We don't talk
between pieces of poem—
holding the thought
over teeth-rattling
potholes—
once nearly hitting
a hot dog cart
on its way
back to Queens.
When you finish
reading
we're nowhere
near home.
We still don't talk.

ON THE NUMBER 6

One day on the way
from 68th to Prince
a blind old man
comes tapping up the car
singing "My Cherie Amour"
shaking a blue paper cup—
"We Are Happy To Serve You" printed
on the front.

When we get to Prince
he passes so close
I see the skin
around his eyes
is wrinkled from squinting
that toothy-confused smile
people make when they go

from a dark place
into the light.
As I get off the car
he gets to the part—
"You're the only one
my heart beats for."
I run up the subway steps
grimacing at the sun.

SNOWFALL

one march morning
while waiting on the platform
a posse of flakes
barreled down
through the grates
landing on
lapels
news-
papers
and
pavement

snow
that had
passed
through
layers of
atmosphere
and
station
structure
its lacy architecture still intact

snow sneaks
snow
won't wake you
when
it
falls
in the night
yet
snow
can
bury
you

THINGS YOU CAN DO WITH A HEART

A group of women
and men
in yoga suits
stood on the lawn
in pairs.

Each one held
a cut-out paper
heart with a
hand-written
message
on the front.

I deserve
to be loved,
said one heart.
I am precious
and important
said another.

Many of the men
and women
were laughing.

Some shouted
their messages
out loud.

One held a heart
that was torn
in two.

HOSPITAL GARDENS

I read in *The New York Times* today
that a group of scientists has discovered
the therapeutic value of hospital gardens.
So instead of sitting in a white room,
one eye on *Jeopardy!*,
squeezing a rubber ball,
the victim of an industrial mishap
plants saplings in Our Lady Of Mercy's back yard.
An expressway casualty is mulching,
an addict tends to blight,
and a man who lost his sight
executes plans to prevent erosion.
Mental patients have been asked to prune,
and at a gathering of wheelchairs,
those unable to wield shears
talk of how they'd trim:
Merely contemplating topiary
encourages recovery.
Gardens are of most use,
the article concludes,
in terminal cases.

ASSISTED LIVING

The Ladies of the League arrange for a volunteer to bring a miniature horse to the old folks' home. "Come see the tiny horse! Now in parking lot B!" the activities director says over the PA system. The residents come with walkers and in wheelchairs to see and touch this unusual animal. Some hold out their hands and let her nuzzle their palms. Others stroke her straw-like mane. All exclaim at how small she is, her withers barely reaching her handler's knees. Imagine a horse so small you have to reach down to touch its head. You would feel like you're living in a fairy tale— and you're the giant. After the handler leaves with the horse, I join my father in the dining room. I look around at the other residents who are bobbing their heads up and down and up and down, gently nickering into their Jell-O.

NATURAL AGING PROCESS

You look inside yourself.
You see ovaries
hardened
to peppercorns.
Tubes:
long black
vanilla beans
hanging in
stoppered
vials.
Your uterus:
a shrunken head.
At your temples
wisps of white hair:
angel wings ready to fly.

ELEGY

My mother wakes up one night, her head feeling like it will burst. She tiptoes into the bathroom careful not to wake my dad. She looks in the mirror. A drop of blood is coming out her nose, then more drops and more till it's a stream, then a blast like that from a fire hose. She yells, "Oh," which wakes my dad who runs in and tells her to tip back her head, which makes the blood shoot up like a geyser and hit the ceiling. He calls the EMTs. At the hospital the doctor tells her that her blood cells are reproducing so fast, her body can't hold them so they're blowing out her nose. Yes, this is cancer and no, there's no cure. The treatment is regularly scheduled phlebotomies. So every two weeks she goes to a place she calls The House of Vampires where they siphon off a few quarts so her nose won't gush at inopportune times. When she says The House of Vampires she laughs like Bela Lugosi. Her only regret is that the blood banks won't take it. "I got bad blood— ba-dum-tsh!" Or, "Gee I feel drained today, ha ha." The more blood they draw, the more jokes she makes. Years pass. I move away. Then one day my dad calls to tell me she doesn't have long to live. I fly out as soon as I can and when I get to her bedside I realize she's gone blind. When she hears my voice, she reaches out and grabs a corner of my jacket. Rubbing it between her fingers she says, "Have I seen this jacket before?"

EVERY YEAR 'BOUT THIS TIME

there's a hum
like a tuning fork hum
like a shift at the late-night factory hum
like the three-party line in a one-horse town hum
like a Singer threading through a bright patch hum
like the workers in the field hum
magnetic field hum
psych ward electro-shock machine hum
it goes hum and then buzz
like the neon sign in the window of the cheap eats buzz
like the bell on the pale green school hall wall buzz
like a locust on the seventeenth spring buzz
like DC current buzz
like alarm clocks buzz
four alarm five alarm thirteen alarm buzz
and like Texas chili it burns
and it bubbles like cheap champagne Nehi Lik-M-Aid
    SweeTARTS Poprocks 2¢ Plain
and it's a thief
takes me from your story
from directions for the bus
from the waiter with the specials of the day
from my own thoughts and it's steady
like the dripdripdrip of nocturnal faucet steady
like bills like barking steady
like taxes traffic junk mail steady
like you nag nag nag
and you can't see it but you feel–
newborn aphids transparent green jumping on the surface
    of the ol' frog pond
blood cells mutant cells lab-grown test cells
jumping on warm glass micro-slides
hopping like popcorn: plastic popper top on the greasy metal kettle

and it teems like a lake teems with fish
like porches with termites
like weevils in the flour bin
like life teems
it's a hum buzz burn dripple dripple burn bubble
    in my mouth from the pollen from the trees in the park
and it's spring

Jeanne-Marie Osterman was born and raised in Everett, Washington. She holds a BA in Italian studies from Gonzaga University, and an MA in linguistics from San Francisco State. Moving to New York City, she worked as an advertising copywriter while studying poetry writing with the late William Packard at NYU, and at the Unterberg Poetry Center at New York's 92nd Street Y. Ms. Osterman's poems have appeared in *Bluestem*, *The Madison Review*, *Third Wednesday*, and other journals. In 2017, she was a finalist for the Levis Prize in Poetry.

www.ingramcontent.com/pod-product-compliance
Lightning Source LLC
LaVergne TN
LVHW041514070426
835507LV00012B/1558